I0157397

THE HILARIOUS SIDE OF PARENTING
Quirky conversations with kids

By Claudia Thomason

Copyright © Claudia Thomason

ISBN – 13: 978-0-9977063-3-8

and

ISBN – 10: 0-9977063-3-3

All rights reserved solely by the author.

All rights reserved. No part of this publication may be reproduced, stored in a retrieval system or transmitted in any form or by any means, electronic, mechanical, including photocopying, recording or otherwise without prior written permission from the author.

All Scripture quotations, unless otherwise indicated, are taken from the Holy Bible, King James Version. Public Domain.

ACKNOWLEDGEMENTS

I gratefully acknowledge the children who spent years in and out of my home, sharing their thoughts with me. They became the source of some of the conversations recorded here.

Some of these sayings are from my children, some were overheard, some were shared with me by family and some were from foster children. I have chosen not to identify them by name, but they all remain in my heart.

To my biological and adopted children, you have been giving me years of material with your quirky sayings and goofy thought processes! Thanks for being exactly who you are.

The material in this book was provided by the members of my extended family, who, thankfully, share a quirky sense of humor.

I

My grateful thanks go to:

Holly Thomason Carter

Derek C. Carter

The Carter Children

Tracy Thomason

The Dance Students in Ms. Tracy's Class

Aaron Thomason, Illustrator

Ed Baker, Editor

And the newest member of the family, Olivia N. Thomason

DEDICATION

This book is dedicated to busy parents everywhere.

Whew! Your job is one that will change the world as you guide your children into adulthood.

Changing the world is hard work! Be sure to take time to laugh for a few minutes each day and recharge your batteries.

Childhood is fleeting in the big picture, but childhood, on a day-to-day basis, may seem to crawl by, giving you more time to love on those kids of yours.

This book is also dedicated to the children who freely talked with us adults and spoke their minds as we listened, interpreted and smiled with them.

Clearly, without them there would be no book.

CONTENTS

In the Beginning

Definitions

And Then There was The End

Epilogue

INTRODUCTION

You have listened as your children, grandchildren, nieces and nephews said cute or funny things or asked off-the-wall questions, haven't you?

Me, too, and I spent decades jotting down the things my children and foster children said.

Granted, I had lots of children living with me over the years, so I had LOTS of material to work with for this book.

Because parenting means your plate is full with the most difficult job ever, I decided to serve up a side dish of laughter.

My goal is to deliver a smile, giving busy parents an opportunity to take a break from making decisions, working on to-do lists, attending meetings and having to be "on" all the time.

Included here is the treasure trove of kids' thoughts I have compiled over several years.

As I worked on pulling the material together, I realized there were no single topics that would fill a chapter. Because kid talk is all over the page, we broke the book into two simple chapters –

the beginning and the end!

Join me as we venture into the minds of children and see the world as they see it.

A merry heart doeth good like a medicine, according to the Bible at Proverbs 17:22. Let's get a hefty dose of that joyful medicine as we laugh together and appreciate the uniqueness of our children.

IN THE BEGINNING

...there were the children:

Me: Would you please put this puzzle in a freezer bag and seal it tightly to keep the pieces together? And be sure to put the picture from the box in there so we know what it is.

Child: Sure.

Me, later: Wow, that bag sure is full for having one little puzzle in it.

Child: That's because I put that puzzle in a bag with the pieces from another puzzle.

Me: So, let me get this straight. You mixed two 500-piece puzzles in one bag? Would you explain to me why that's a good idea?

Child, proudly: Because now, two people can work the puzzle at the same time!

(Free to first caller: 1,000-piece puzzle. Practically new.)

Child: What does a fermatavor do?

Me: Fer-ma-ta-vor. Hmmm, even when I say it slowly, I'm not too sure what that is. Will you use it in a sentence?

Child: Okay. "It is a fermatavor."

Me. Ummm, that doesn't quite do it for me. Maybe you could draw a picture for me. Or point to it.

Child: Here it is, she said, pointing out the patio door. At the thermometer.

I suggested 10 minutes quiet time for questionable behavior. A few minutes later, the conversation went like this:

Child: I'm done now, right? It's been 10 minutes.

Me: No, it hasn't. It's been 5.

Child: Okay, I won't argue about it. Just let me say that women tell time a lot different than men!

(I'd be willing to bet that is not the last time in your life you will hear yourself say that, little man.)

What would you like to be when you grow up?

I wanted to be a police woman when I grew up because of the whistle.

Do you still want to be a police woman?

No, I forgot about the bad guys!

This child can't make up her mind:

Child: I can't stop deciding!

Child: My aunt could cook! When she took a roll of hot pans out of the oven, mmmm, it smelled so good!

Me: Was that possibly a pan of hot rolls that smelled so good?

Child: Oh, yeah, haha.

Child: I am going to leave.

Me: Leave?

Child: Yes, run away.

Me: Oh. Well, I will miss you terribly.

Child: I am going anyway.

Me: That makes me sad, but I guess I could help you pack. How can I help?

Child: You can pack up some food for me.

Me: Oh, I'm sorry. You can't take the food. If you take the food, there won't be any here for the rest of us.

Child: Seriously?

Me: I'm afraid so. What else can I do?

Child: You can give me a suitcase.

Me: Oh, I'm sorry. There are no suitcases to spare. We may be taking another trip to Texas or somewhere after you leave, and we will need them.

Child: Seriously? Then you can put my toys in a trash bag for me.

Me: Oh, I'm sorry. We only have four trash bags left. If you take one, we won't have enough to make it through the rest of the month.

Child: How am I supposed to carry my toys then?

Me, making a big circle with my arms: Like this, I guess.

Child: Seriously? Running away is too much trouble. I'm going outside and play.

(Whew! Another major crisis averted along the rocky path of childhood.)

This thoughtful child colored a little picture for a fly on the window:

Child: Here you go baby fly, I made you a baby newspaper!

One sunny day on a walk with his Mama, a child started doing a frenzied dance, waving his arms, shaking his legs and shouting:

Child: Aggghhhh! Get it off me! Make it go away! Help!

Me: What? Do you have a bug on you? I don't see it.

Child, becoming hysterical: No, that, that, hopping up and down, waving his arms and shouting.

Me: Help me out here. Point to what is on you so I can help.

Child, bending over: That! That! Under my shoes, he said pointing to his shadow seemingly connected to the bottom of his feet.

Do I have to do my chores today before I watch a movie?

Yes, you need to get your chores done.

But I can do them after the movie.

They are to be done first. It's not negotiable.

What's "negotiable" mean?

It means I'm not
going to discuss it.

But you are.

I'm trying to be
polite.

If you were polite, you
would let me watch a
movie first!

11

Ms. Tracy, the patient dance teacher, and her new class: My name is Ms. Tracy.

Children: Can we call you Ms. T?

Ms. T: Yes, you can call me that. Okay today we're going to...

Children: Can we call you Ms. Turtle?

Ms. T: As much as I like that, let's stick with Ms. Tracy or Ms. T. Are there any questions before we get started?

Children: Can we just make a list of names to call you that start with a T?

Ms. T: That really sounds like fun, but why don't we cheer instead?

Children: Can we cheer for Ms. Tutu?

Ms. T: Sigh... You bet. Let's warm up.

Sometimes the adults in the home give the kids lots of material to work with. This was one instance.

Setting the scene: I decided to try the new wrinkle smoothing cream a friend had given me in an unmarked jar. I wouldn't have purchased it myself because giving wrinkles the boot is not cheap. It looked a little too white and somewhat thick to me. I mixed it with a darker color makeup. As I smoothed it on, I noticed it had a nice bouquet – a little like fresh mint leaves. Nice touch, I thought. I walked out to the kitchen where the little people were having breakfast.

Child: What's up with your face?

Me: Nothing. Why?

Child: Because you look like a ghost.

Me: No, this is an expensive new product I am trying. (Doing my best to sound clever, even though the solution had begun to burn my eyes.)

Child: You better take another look because I think you spent way too much for that new stuff.

Me: Oh, you are so funny. I'll be right back.

13

I hurried to the bathroom to get this cream out of my eyes. I glanced in the drawer and saw my make up right on top and beside it was the wrinkle smoother. No, wait. My eyes were burning, but I squinted to look at the jar again. The Child was right. My friend taped a label to the jar which I didn't see. Apparently, I had managed to cover my face, eyes and all, in a mixture of Beautiful Buff makeup and a homemade concoction of whitening toothpaste with peppermint essential oils. I cleaned it off and went back to the kitchen.

Me: I'm so sorry. You were right about the cream. It was a mistake.

Child: Whatever you did to fix it didn't work either. You look like you just swallowed fire.

(He just shook his head every time he glanced my way the rest of the day.)

Child: Is my grandma going to be okay? They took her lungs out, right?

Me: No, they didn't take her lungs out. You don't live if they take your lungs out.

Child: Yes you do. My friend had her lungs taken out and she got better.

Me: I doubt that they took her lungs out.

Child, not one to back down on any issue: Yes, they did!

(Long pause)

Child: Oh, wait. It was her tonsils. Yes, they took her tonsils out, and she was fine.

(Nice moms don't say, "I told you so." So I won't. At least not to her face.)

Child: I'm all dressed for school. I'm going to make breakfast now.

Me, from another room: Okay, I'm coming out to fix your toast.

Child, staring at me as I entered the room: Did you do your hair yet? Because if you did, you are having a REALLY bad hair day!

(What a confidence builder she is!)

Young mom, waking up a small child for breakfast, hears:

I'm trying to sleep. I have my eyes folded.

Dance Teacher Ms. Tracy's cheer class:

Child 1: Ms. Tracy, these pom poms are hard to hold.

Child 2: They itch our hands.

Child 1. They make our palms sweaty

Child 2: Why don't they have handles?

Ms. Tracy: Handles cost more money.

Child 1, clasping her pomp poms together dramatically at her chest: Please, Ms. Tracy! Think of the children!

Child: Daddy, I want to tell Mommy a secret. You need to go to a happy place. Go jump on a rainbow.

Mom, talking with a little girl after bedtime prayers:

Mom: Jesus is always with us.

Child: Where? I don't see him.

Mom: He's in our hearts.

Child: Oh! I feel him right here, pointing to right side of her chest. Oh! Now he's right here, patting the center of her chest. He's just moving all around in there!

Me: It's Chili Cook Off day at church on Sunday. I need to get the crock pot out for the pot luck.

Child: I know what's a crock pot, but what's a crock pot luck?

Me: It's called pot luck. A pot luck is where everyone brings some food, and we all share.

Child: Share? My food?

Me: Yes.

Child: Really? I don't think so.

Me: But that's the idea.

Child: I probably shouldn't go. I'm not so good at sharing.

Mom: Are you okay back there son?

Child struggling to stay awake in the back seat: I'm trying to tell my eyes to stay open and not go to sleep!

(He was asleep before the words left his mouth.)

Frequently I have kids with a wild, crazy spirit of adventure come to live with me. This apparently wasn't one of them.

I'm bored.

Did you finish your homework? And pick up the things from the bedroom floor? And put your shoes away?

Yeah. Now I'm bored.

You can go outside and kick the soccer ball around, or play with the tetherball, or hunt for cicada shells.

No, I'm just gonna lay down on the floor and look at the ceiling for a few minutes.

And that's not going to be boring?

You be sure to do that.

I don't think so. I'll let you know.

In science class, a child was learning about the skin, bacteria and viruses. Coincidentally, she was also battling a runny nose and had, unbeknownst to me, put her used tissue on the table.

Me: Oh, oh! You need to pick up everything from your side of the table now so it can be wiped down with Clorox.

Child: Why?

Me: Think about it for a minute. What will you be leaving behind now on the table (referring to germs from her tissue)?

Child: I don't know, but I think it's epidermis?

Child: My hands are dancing, just not my feet. These are happy tears ... sometimes my tears are happy and are not just sad! That's why my hands are dancing.

(I cannot begin to understand what that child was trying to say.)

When I no longer need my van, I think I will get a VW convertible.

A convertible?

Yes. I used to have one and I loved it!

That's not you.

What do you mean?

You're too old for a convertible. You need to keep your van.

21

Dinner is ready. Please wash up.

okay. I want to say your cooking has gotten a lot better lately.

Better than what?

Better than when I came.

I was trying to impress you when you came. Now we are eating food purchased at a warehouse store for a song.

Then that makes you cheap and a good cook!

(I assume he means cheap in a good way, like frugal.)

Ms. Tracy, dance teacher.

Child: Ms. Tracy, I have a paper cut.

Ms. T: Do you need a Band-Aid?

Child: Yes, see?

Ms. Tracy, retrieving a tiny plastic first aid kit from her backpack: Here we go.

Child: She has a real medicine box! She's a doctor and a cheerleader!

Child raving about her new pants:

I LOVE these pants. They have a waistable adjustband!

In the restaurant rest room:

Child striking a pose by the wall: Dad, do you know why I'm standing like this?

Dad: No, Son. Why are you standing like that?

Child: Because I want to look awesome! This is how the boys stand when they want to look awesome!

(Nothing gets by these impressionable little kids!)

———————————————————

Me at Christmas time: We have three trees. One is for you to trim because I have done the others.

Child: I have a tree? Of my own?

Me: Yes, I have already put the lights and the polka dot ribbon on it. Would you like to hang the ornaments now?

Child: Yes!

She hung ornaments on her three-foot tree. We turned on the tiny colored lights and stepped back to admire our work.

Me: Great job! We are all done.

Child: What do you mean, we are all done? We are going to trim the tree, aren't we?

Me: Yes, we did that. All the spots on the trees are full of pretty sparkly things.

Child, her anxiety level visibly rising with each carefully-chosen word: But. You. Said. We. Would. Trim. It. Trim it. Trim it. We didn't trim it!

Me: Will you show me what you mean by "trimming" the tree?

Child, raising her arm to sweep across the top third of each tree, making the ear-splitting sound of a buzz saw: THIS is trimming!

(It kind of disturbs me that she knows more about buzz saws than decorating Christmas trees.)

ALL I WANT IS A PIECE OF QUIET!!

When I opened the drinking glass cupboard, a glass tumbled to the counter, smashing into tiny pieces.

Child: Why did you do that?

Me: I didn't mean to, but someone stacked the glasses weird. Again.

Child: That's okay. When you open my Christmas present ...

Me: WAIT! It's supposed to be a surprise. Don't tell me.

Child: Okay, I won't, but you will still have the same number of glasses. (Wink. Wink.)

(I hope I remember never to tell this one a secret.)

Child: Do you have a dollar I can have?

Me: Sure. What for?

Child: We can dress down on Fridays at school if we bring a dollar to donate to the senior class.

Me: I see. Do you have a dollar?

Child: No.

Me: I think you might because you just got your allowance.

Child: You are supposed to get that kind of necessary stuff for me. My allowance is for other fun stuff.

(Since when did dressing down on Fridays become "necessary stuff?")

While reading the story about the game of jacks from my book, Kindergarten Lessons I Learned in Africa, to one of the children:

Child: Is jacks the game with those silver things and a ball?

Me, nodding my head: Jacks

Child: Yeah, is jacks that game with those silver things and a ball?

Me: Yes. Jacks.

Child, walking away, sighing: Never mind. I'll figure it out myself.

(You're not off to a good start, little one.)

Child reporting on health class from school:

Child: I learned it is important to use condiments so you don't transmit diseases.

Me: Pardon me?

Child: Condiments. Is that the right word?

(Probably not.)

Little Visiting Person: I love you so much. I feel sorry for you because you only have two TVs. We have one in the living room, one in the couch room, one in the bedroom, one in mom's bedroom, and one in sister's bedroom.

Me: That's nice of you to be thinking about me, but I really only need two televisions. And I don't really even need them.

Child: You're just saying that so you don't look poor.

(Thanks, I'm always pleased to find out why I say the stuff I do.)

Did you make your bed?

I didn't know I had to. You didn't tell me.

Not in the last 20 minutes I haven't, but it is a given.

I will give you this amazing picture if you will make my bed for me.

I will trade today, but you need to make your own bed from now on.

I will.

Me: Right about now, I need some quiet time. Will you please take some quiet time too?

Child: I don't want to, but I will. But I don't want to.

Me: Thank you. I appreciate it.

Child, calling from her room: I'm trying to be quiet, but I might have to swallow! Will that be too much noise for you?

Me, finding my bracelet on the kitchen counter: Oh, look, someone found my little gold bracelet.

Child: It was on the closet floor.

Me: It must have slipped off my wrist when I was cleaning the closet.

Child: I think it probably fell off because it is an ankle bracelet.

Me: What makes you think it's an ankle bracelet?

Child: Well, duh. Look at the size.

Me: Sadly, it looks like a bracelet to me.

Child, putting her skinny little arm up so I could see her wrist:

That would go around my wrist TWICE.

(Yeah, well, we're not all built like you, but thanks for the constant reminders.)

Emmy, you are so tall! I think you grew another foot while I was gone!

No, Grandma. I still only has two feet!

Me: Did I hear you say you are studying Greek mythology in school?

Child: Yes. The Greek gods and goddesses.

Me: I studied that in high school. We had a special club after school to read Greek mythology. The Advanced Reading Team, I think it was called.

Child, laughing: Only then it was current events, right?

Me: Heh-heh, cute. It's called mythology for a reason. What are you learning?

Child: Zeus, the god of lightening; Poseidon, god of the sea; Hades, the underworld. And goddesses like Athena, the goddess of wisdom. So, I bet you met them in person back then, huh?

Me: Ugh. There's only so much of this slapstick I can take, kid. I'm going to go start dinner.

Child: What's slapstick?

(I give up.)

Dinner table talk:

Child: You know what I miss?

Me: No, what?

Child: I miss the conversations at the table at my friend's house. Her whole family is really intelligent. Everyone was interesting. I miss that.

(I don't believe I've ever had my conversational skills discounted so thoroughly.)

Dad: What do you want to drink?

Child 1: Milk

Dad: Milk what? What's the other word? Daughter, help him out.

Child 2: CHOCOLATE milk.

Dad: Um...No. The word I'm looking for is PLEASE ... milk PLEASE!

(I guess there's more work to be done.)

Child to exhausted mom after a 45-minute temper tantrum: My tears are all done.

(I'd be willing to bet so is mom's patience.)

Putting a scarf over the face of a Child before he went out to catch the bus:

Me: Let's see, I will wrap this around your nose and mouth and tie it in back.

Child, hissing and singing the Star Wars theme through the scarf: I AM YOUR FATHER.

Me: What? I thought this was like Ralphie's brother, Randy, in "A Christmas Story."

Child: What? Who's Ralphie?

(Sigh. The Christmastime generation gap played out by front doors everywhere.)

I was sitting on the kitchen floor when the Child walked in. It had been THAT kind of day.

Child: What are you doing?

Me: Trying to decide what to have for lunch.

Child: But you are sitting in the middle of the floor with a can of whipped cream in your hand.

Me: Yes, yes I am.

Child: I don't see any lunch.

Me: The question I am deciding is if I am going to have two blasts of whipped cream for lunch or if I am going to get up and actually make myself something nutritious.

Child: I would vote for the whipped cream if I was you. And can I eat with you?

Me: Have you had a hard day too?

Child: Yes.

Me: Then okay, let's do this. We will make a real lunch afterward.

(Some days are just whipped-cream-for-lunch-days. Wouldn't you agree?)

After demonstrating new choreography to a group of K-4 students:

Ms. Tracy: Does anyone have any questions before I turn on the music?

Child: Can we order pizza for us? I'm starving!

Young mom to daughter struggling with writing her lessons:

Mom: I'm sorry to see you're sad. I can see you are crying.

Child: Yes.

Mom: Are you going to be okay so we can talk?

Child, wiping tears from her eyes: Yes, but my eyes is still melting.

Ms. Tracy, did you teach another class right before us because your hair looks freaky!

No, I just didn't pull it back into a ponytail today like usual.

Because it looks freaky.

~* Sigh *~

I heard you. Thanks for letting me know.

Child: If I saw a rattlesnake, I would, um, I would ... OH, YEAH! I would stop drop and roll!

Me: Hmmm, why would you do that?

Child: Seriously? To get away from the rattlesnake.

Me: You better hope you and the snake are rolling in opposite directions.

Child, after a long pause: Oh, now I remember. You stop drop and roll if you are on fire. You run from snakes.

(I'm glad we worked this out before you encounter that next snake.)

Me: I can see what you are doing, you know.

Child: You can't see me. You are looking at the cat.

Me: Remember how I taught you that you don't have to be looking directly at something to see it?

Child: No.

Me: Remember we talked about peripheral vision and I can ....

Child: Oh yeah. You can see me out of your middle eye!

(That's just creepy)

Child, coming in from outside: Mmmm, something smells really good.

Me: You aren't usually that enthusiastic about my cooking, so thank you.

Child: What are you cooking?

Me: Pot holders.

Child: Pot holders? What are pot holders?

Me: Things that you pick up hot pots with.

Child: Oh. I don't think I have ever had that for dinner.

Me: Me neither. I just cook them. I don't eat them.

(Note to self: Remember to remove the pot holder from the lid before turning on the burner.)

Young child: I am going to run far away today.

Me: Really? Why would you do that?

Child: To show you how fast I am.

Me: Oh, I thought you were running away.

Child: I am.

Me: Where will you run that is very far away?

Child, scanning the room for the farthest point she could see, incorporating the highest number in her world: I am running to Fifty-two-ty corner. That's far!

(The corner was as far as she could imagine in her little world, and 52 was a number she remembered from playing with her mischievous brother who mercilessly taught her 52 card pickup.)

Child: Is that your driver's license? Can I see it?

Me: Sure.

Child: Wow! You sure were young. It must have been taken a long time ago.

(Actually, it was taken two months before this child came into my life. Apparently, I aged quickly after that.)

Child: Look mom! I found my toy. I must have been extracted last time I put my toys away.

Mom: A little distracted, right?

Child: I shouldn't get so frustrated. I should have more patiences when I'm looking for something I can't find.

(If you figure out how to do that, teach me please.)

Hey! Dinner smells great! DID YOU BUY IT?

Dinnertime conversations can be the highlight of the day when the children talk so fast that their brains can't keep up with their mouths. For instance:

Child 1: I love that stuff!

Child 2: What is it?

Child 1: Beetles and noof.

Me: Oh, I hope not.

Child 2: What is it?

Me: Noodles and beef.

Child: Look what I found outside (holding up a long, fat, clearly dead creepy crawler of some kind)

Me: Amazing. Take it outside.

Child: But look what I found. It's a caterpillar. It will turn into a butterfly.

Me: Take it outside. It is a grub of some kind and it will turn into something, but it isn't going to be a butterfly.

45

Child: But I found it. It's dead. It will become a butterfly soon.

Me: Dead things generally don't turn into anything except dust. Put it under the trees so if it does wake up as something else, it will have something to eat. But get it out of the house.

Child after playing outside for a few minutes: Guess what? Since it was dead, we dissected it. It was cool.

Me: What? Here use baby wipes then go wash with hot water and soap. And change your clothes.

(Ugggg. Kid care isn't for the faint of heart.)

Her little siblings formed a band and were marching around with toy instruments, playing a wild tune.

Child: Look Mom! We are the Banders!

(Kind of like the one-hit wonders.)

Overheard at Dance Class:

Child: Mom, what's wrong with your face?

Mom: I'm trying a new lipstick. So, that's a no on the red then, right?

———————————————————

Child: School was fun today. I played volleyball in gym class.

Me: Sounds fun. I really liked volleyball in school.

Child, dripping with sarcasm: They had volleyball back then?

Me: Yes. As a matter of fact, I was on our elementary school team. We got to travel to other schools and play their teams.

Child laughing: Is that when they had the cloth balls that unraveled when you spiked them?

Me: No, they were more like bowling balls and you had to be really, really good to get them over the net.

Child: Wow!

(I'm not above a little sarcasm myself.)

Mom was nicely redirecting a child who had hit another one with a toy. She was pleased that she had her rapt attention. It went like this:

Mom: So, you understand that we need to be kind to each other and not hit?

Child: (Nods head yes, and intently watches mom.)

Mom: That's really good. Now can you go over there and say you are sorry for that?

Child: (Nodding head, very focused on mom.)

Me: Okay, I will go with …

Child: Mommy! You gots the same earrings as the Pirate Fairies! But they only gots one.

(Mom would be kidding herself if she thought daughter heard anything she said.)

How come you're so nice today?

You expected me to be mean, maybe?

Well, no, but mom said when she was little, you were a little cranky with her.

I know I look old to you, but I am not your mom's mother. I am her friend.

Oh, that's why you're so nice today.

The child came out for breakfast with her hair looking a bit like the little boy on the Dutch Boy Paints cans. Except short in front and long in back.

Me: When did you cut your hair?

Child: I didn't. I looked like this yesterday.

Me: Well, this is the first time you have not worn a pony tail all week, so I couldn't tell about your hair until today. When did you cut it?

Child: I didn't cut it. Don't you get it? You need new glasses because I didn't cut my hair.

Me: I think you are protesting too much. I don't want to argue about it, but you remember you get one consequence for breaking a rule and one more each time you lie about it. Want to tell the truth?

Child, stomping away: I didn't cut my hair. You can't even see I didn't cut my hair (as bedroom door slams).

Me: When you are under control, come out and finish breakfast so you can start on chores. Don't forget to empty the trash.

Child: I know, I know, I know.

Me, later: Here, let me help you with your trash from your bathroom. Hmmm, what's this at the bottom of the trash? Clumps of hair? Bwahahaha! You are so busted!

(Another mature parenting moment at our house.)

Quickly backing out of the driveway for appointments in town, I glanced in the rearview mirror to confirm that everyone had seat belts on. Locking eyes with the shortest child in the back seat, I heard:

Child: "Oh. Eye shadow."

Me: "Yes. Why?"

Child: Enthusiastically strumming an air guitar. "Well, you look like a rock star! A cool rocker!"

(Ugh. I am apparently on my way to several professional appointments looking like a rock star.)

Ah! The cat is going to throw up!

I'm going to be a fireman when I throw up.

The power went out during a storm after everyone was in bed. The nightlights, of course, went out too.

Child: Mommy! Help me! Help me open my eyes. I can't get my eyes open. Help!

Me, going into the room holding a flashlight: I am sorry you are frightened. Can you see my flashlight?

Child: Yes.

Me: That means your eyes are open. It is just too dark to see anything. How about if I leave my flashlight with you tonight?

(Sometimes you just want to chuckle, but that would be so insensitive in a crisis like this.)

Child: I think I have a boyfriend.

Me: We have talked about this. You're too young for a boyfriend.

Child: But he really wants me for his girlfriend.

Me: That's nice. You're still too young.

Child, whining: But IKTOIFMF.

Me: Please don't talk in code unless the translation is inappropriate. Then don't tell me at all.

Child: I Know This One Is For Me Forever.

(Wow! In Junior High I was lucky if I knew how to find the room for my next class. Knowing a fact as large as your forever partner is huge. And unreliable. She was whining about someone else the next week.)

Child: My back hurts.

Me: I'm sorry. What happened?

Child: I was under my bed, and I decided to stand up.

Me, trying not to laugh: What makes you think you can stand up under your bed?

Child: Well, I guess I can't. But I wanted to try.

(Four broken slats later, we know we can't stand up under the bed. Painful example of learning a lesson the hard way.)

Mom, I want that played shirt here in the picture. See it?

Yes, I see it. But it's pronounced "plaid."

That doesn't make any sense.

Welcome to the English language.

At dinner, we have a ritual that we say our highs and lows for the day, with something nice about each other and ourselves.

Child: Something I like about (Child 1) is that when they aren't mad, they are nice. Something I like about Claudia is that she is a good cook sometimes. (I can't seem to be able to outrun my cooking reputation!)

Me: Okay, thanks. How about something you like about you?

Child: I don't know anything.

Me: Think hard about the qualities that you like about yourself.

Child struggling: I don't like anything about myself. Maybe that my socks don't match. I like that a lot.

(Not exactly what I was going for, but we'll take it.)

It had cooled down to about 80 on the patio and this child wanted to play restaurant. She put on her skates, grabbed a tablet and pen and skated around "taking orders" from make believe people.

Me: I think I will stop for a cold drink. Do you have a chair for another customer?

Child: Yes. Please come in. We are so happy you are here. What would you like ma'am?

Me: I think I would just like something cold to drink. What's that orange slushee drink called with the ice cream in it?

Child: I think you should eat something.

Me: Oh, no thank you. I will just have that cold drink.

Child: No, I will bring you a hamburger with mustard and mayo. And corn on the cob.

Me: Really, I just want something to drink.

Child: You are getting a hamburger. And corn on the cob.

Me: Seriously, I don't think wait staff does that. Anywhere. Ever.

Child, getting excited and flailing around on her skates, arms flapping like a bird: Well, we do that here.

Me: Hmmm. Okay, if you promise it is really good, you may bring me food with my drink. What is the name of that orange slushee drink with the ice cream?

Child: I don't know. I'll call it IRIS.

Me: And why not?

Child: One hamburger, corn on the cob and orange slushee IRIS coming up. That will be two cents.

(Except for the pushy wait staff, this place is outstanding!)

Child: Remember the shiny silver jingle bell you let me hold?

Me: Yes. Are you done with it? May I have it to put it away?

Child: Probably not.

Me: Why not?

Child: I wondered what it would sound like if I put it in my mouth. And jumped around.

Me: Okay. How did it sound ... and where is it?

Child: That's the funny thing. It didn't make much noise. Then it was gone.

Me: Gone?

Child: I swallowed it. I don't hear it when I jump though. Even with my mouth open.

(The doctor said it would take a couple days, but to watch for it and that it would show up eventually.)

We are big on using our coping skills around here. Combine that with the resident queen of duct tape, and it gets interesting. The scene: I poured everyone a glass of almond milk for dinner.

Child: I don't like almond milk or soy milk. I said I wanted regular milk.

Me: At the store in front of the dairy case, we heard you say you wanted almond milk. All we have now is soy milk or almond milk. Take your choice. Or don't have milk.

Child stomping away: I told you regular milk, regular milk, regular milk. Don't you get it?

Me: Apparently not.

Child later, sporting a huge hunk of duct tape over her mouth: Mmmlldttdllttt ...

Me: Not sure what you are trying to tell me.

Child, ripping off the tape: It's my coping skill so I don't keep saying things I shouldn't.

Me: You do know that good choices come from within you and require very few props, but I applaud the effort.

Child: My slippers are sleeping, but when I wiggle them, they will wake up.

(Animated slippers. Awesome. Now if they can just get the kids up in time for school, that would be great. A little freaky, but great.)

Me: What is in your pockets?

Child: Nothing. Just some jelly beans and stuff.

Me: Maybe you better show me. It looks like you may have taken all the jelly beans from the bowl at my friend's house today.

Child: I did because we don't have any at home. And they had lots.

Me, inspecting the sticky jelly beans covered with disgusting pocket lint: You do know that is wrong and might be called stealing?

Child: No, stealing is taking stuff that doesn't belong to you. She gave me the jelly beans.

Me: Not all of them.

Child: Then she shouldn't have held the dish out and asked me if I wanted them.

(Kids are so literal.)

Child: "Valentimes" Day is for lovin' and giving hearts.

Daddy and Mommy: Aw, that's sweet. If we could, we would give you the moon, baby girl.

Child: I can get it Daddy.

Daddy: You can?

Child: Yes Daddy. If you put me on your shoulders, I can pull down the moon for you!

(Seriously, somebody ought to write a song about that!)

Child in the back seat of car: Excuse me. Excuse me. EXCUSE ME!

Me: If you are trying to get my attention, I'm pretty sure you know my name.

Child: Yes, but Excuse Me is easier to remember than Claudia.

Me: I get that. I was 5 before I even remembered my own name.

Child: Really?

Me: Yep. What did you want?

Child: I forgot.

(Later) Child: Excuse me. Excuse me. EXCUSE ME!

(Sigh. I guess I don't need to win this one today.)

At dance rehearsal.

Child, on stage: I don't want to do it.

Ms. T: Well, you have two choices. You can take your spot over there or you can sit in the audience, but you have to decide right now.

Child: If I sit in the audience will I still get my sucker?

Ms. T: No, but what if you just try the first dance and if you don't like it then you can go sit down.

Child: Then will I get my sucker?

Ms. T: No, but maybe if you try the first dance you will end up liking them all and earn your sucker. Can you try?

Child marched over to his spot the on stage and performed the entire show with gusto.

(Moral: Never underestimate the draw of a Dum Dum.)

Child was supposed to be doing homework at the table but was instead playing with one of those little squares that have pieces in them that you move around to make a face or spell words. He got caught.

Me: I have asked you to put that down a dozen times.

Child: What? I don't have anything.

Me: Give it to me.

Child: What? I don't have anything.

Me, snatching at it when he let his guard down: Give it to me.

Child, tossing the toy over his shoulder into the living room: Run Mr. Smiley Face, run!

(I watched it roll away, and to my great chagrin, I began to laugh. His quick wit wins again.)

DEFINITIONS

How about if we close this out by giving you a list of definitions, approved and used by kids. Feel free to use them if you are ever at a loss for words.

They are especially impressive if you use them at board meetings and when speaking to large audiences:

Food:

Frabeebee	Strawberry
Oak	Inside of an egg
Kabosan	Kielbasa
Oatmeat	Oatmeal
Toter Tales	Tater Tots

Feelings:

Exoti	Anxiety
Obnauseus	Obnoxious

Animals:

Awdor	Otter
Sea tratel	Sea turtle
Kaguroow	Kangaroo
Jagwater	Jaguar
Envelope	Antelope

Our bodies:

Pitbulls in her eyes	Pupils
Sprinkles	Freckles
Taptoo	Tattoo
Tinky fweet	Stinky feet
Eye-a-bowels	Eyeballs
Pedicule	Cuticle

Feet nails   Toe nails

Prayers:

Thank you, Jesus, God our Father, once again. Amen

God bless the firefighters, the police, the soldiers and the people in the hurricanes and floods. Mom? Will everyone be okay tonight?

At home:

Ikter Dishner   Air conditioner

Frog toads   Toad stools

Pawprin   Apron

Life serve   Life Savers

Rimottitter   Room monitor

Kunicle   Mechanical (pencil)

Fermatador   Thermometer

Just for fun:

Amblanx	Ambulance
Feet Sleeves	Pant legs
Crock pot	Pot Luck
A fountain to pee in	Urinal
Globes	Gloves
Compversation	Conversation
Veins on wrist	Colors from my Crayons
Side by down	Upside down
Up side up	Right side up
Dehale	Deflate

AND THEN THERE WAS THE END

This story is called "Gaggles and Herds and Littles of Kittens" and can be found in the blog section of www.claudiathomason. com with other Little People stories:

Child: Wow! We were so lucky to see all those gooses go to the lake yesterday...Goose? Gooses?

Me: Geese

Child: Yeah, a heard of geese.

Me. Gaggle.

Child: Oh, yeah, a gaggle. And then I saw a gaggle of antelope on the way home.

Me: Well, that's a herd.

Child: Yeah, herd. Look, look up in the sky, it is a gaggle of birds all together!

Me: Flock.

Child: Flock? Oh, yeah, flock. And you told me it is a little of kittens and puppies.

Me: Litter. You are really good at remembering, little one.

EPILOGUE

Children's stories never really end. As long as kids are talking, they will be saying funny things.

I would love to hear your family's stories. There are so many kids telling so many funny stories and saying great things that there should be a second book like this. If you are willing to share your family's short stories and quotes, I'll review them for a future book. If your story is selected, you'll be sent a permission form well in advance of publication of the book to assure you still wish the story to be included. You and your child will, of course, retain the rights to your material and be given credit in the book for your funny story.

Won't that be fun to see your child or grandchild's best story in print?

Here's how to make that happen.

Simply send me an email to info@ claudiathomason.com and share your funny story. Be sure to include your name, your child's first name and age, your best email address and phone number, and your funny story. That's it.

Don't have a funny story? That's okay! Send me an email if you want to be on the list to get notice when the next Hilarious Side of Parenting book is ready to be published! If you enjoyed the stories in this book, you are my kind of person, and I don't want to lose track of you. Your email can say you want notice of the next book and that's it.

Let's keep laughing. Would you like to get another funny kid story in your email a couple times a month? Sign up for our free "Three-Minute Newsletter for Busy Parents." We include a fresh story, some parenting tips and wrap up with a take-away for parenting or for life in general.

Visit http://claudiathomason.com/sign-free-newsletter/ to be added to our list.

I'm looking forward to hearing from you!

www.ingramcontent.com/pod-product-compliance
Lightning Source LLC
Chambersburg PA
CBHW060142050426
42448CB00010B/2252